Y0-CMH-082

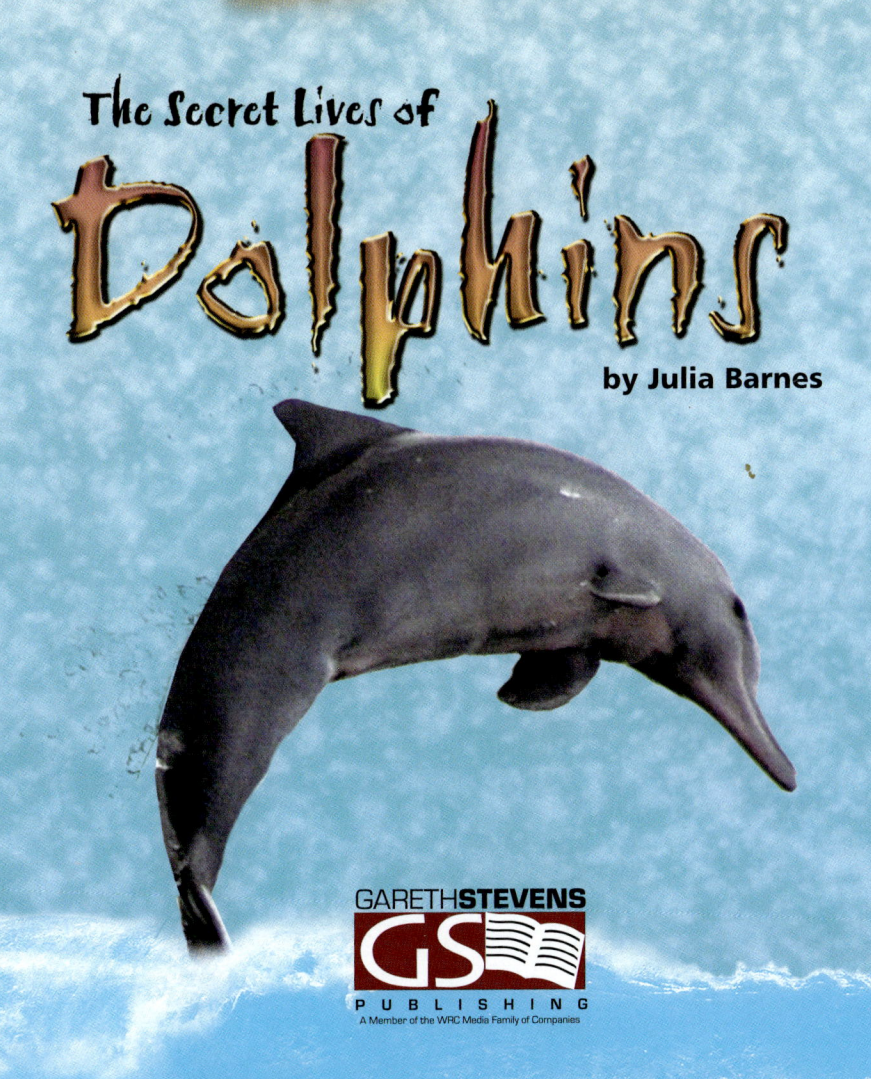

The SECRET LIVES of Animals

The Secret Lives of Dolphins

by Julia Barnes

GARETH STEVENS
GS
PUBLISHING
A Member of the WRC Media Family of Companies

Please visit our web site at: www.garethstevens.com
For a free color catalog describing Gareth Stevens Publishing's list of high-quality books
and multimedia programs, call 1-800-542-2595 (USA) or 1-800-387-3178 (Canada).
Gareth Stevens Publishing's fax: (414) 332-3567.

Library of Congress Cataloging-in-Publication Data

Barnes, Julia, 1955-
   The secret lives of dolphins / Julia Barnes.
      p. cm. — (The secret lives of animals)
   Includes bibliographical references and index.
   ISBN-13: 978-0-8368-7656-7 (lib. bdg.)
   1. Dolphins—Juvenile literature. I. Title.
QL737.C432B385   2007
599.53—dc22   2006035323

This North American edition first published in 2007 by
Gareth Stevens Publishing
A Member of the WRC Media Family of Companies
330 West Olive Street, Suite 100
Milwaukee, WI 53212 USA

This edition copyright © 2007 by Gareth Stevens, Inc.
Original edition copyright © 2006 by Westline Publishing.
Additional end matter copyright 2007 by Gareth Stevens, Inc.

Gareth Stevens editor: Gini Holland
Gareth Stevens designer: Kami M. Strunsee
Gareth Stevens art direction: Tammy West
Gareth Stevens production: Jessica Yanke and Robert Kraus

Photo credits: copyright © istockphoto.com: Christian Gude pp. 1, 8; Rosespetal p. 9; Chad Breece
p.10; Joe Stone p. 12; Ian Harvey p. 13; Craig Tuttle p. 15; Ben Hodgson p. 18; Jose Antonio Fernandez
p. 19; Evgeniya Lazareva p. 21; Andrew Howe p. 22; Tom Hirtreiter p. 23; Steve Serowka p. 24;
Blair Howard p. 25; p. Ian Harvey p. 26; Matty Symons p. 27; Karen Roach p. 28; Craig Tuttle p. 29.
All other images copyright © Westline Publishing Limited.

All rights reserved. No part of this book may be reproduced, stored in a retrieval system,
or transmitted in any form or by any means, electronic, mechanical, photocopying,
recording, or otherwise, without the prior written permission of the copyright holder.

Printed in the United States of America

1 2 3 4 5 6 7 8 9 10 10 09 08 07 06

Contents

INTRODUCING THE DOLPHIN	4
THE WAYS OF DOLPHINS	6
THE DOLPHIN'S PERFECT BODY	8
HOW A DOLPHIN SEES THE WORLD	10
DISCOVERING SPECIAL SKILLS	12
WHAT DOES A DOLPHIN DO ALL DAY?	14
HOW DO DOLPHINS COMMUNICATE?	16
TIMES OF TROUBLE	20
WHEN DOLPHINS ARE READY TO BREED	22
THE FAMILY LIFE OF DOLPHINS	24
THE CALVES GROW UP	26
DOLPHINS AND PEOPLE	28
GLOSSARY	30
MORE BOOKS TO READ/WEB SITES	31
INDEX	32

Introducing the Dolphin

Intelligent, acrobatic, and playful, the dolphin is one of the most spectacular animals of the ocean. It has been hard for people to find out what life is like for animals that live deep underwater. How does a dolphin spend its days? How do dolphins communicate with each other? Do they spend much time with their offspring? What do they eat? To find out about dolphins, we need to enter their secret world.

SECRETS OF SUCCESS

More than two-thirds of the Earth's surface is covered in water. The first living creatures were found in the sea. About 400 to 360 million years ago, four-legged animals emerged from the sea to live on the land.

As land animals developed, a family group left the land to return to the sea. These first water **mammals** appeared about thirty-four million years ago. They had long bodies, and their hind limbs were very short.

It took a long time for water mammals to adapt to their new environment, but by ten million years ago, the water mammal family had split into **whales**, dolphins, and **porpoises** — the only mammals that can live permanently in the sea.

The whale (*top*) and the dolphin (*bottom*) are both ocean mammals called cetaceans.

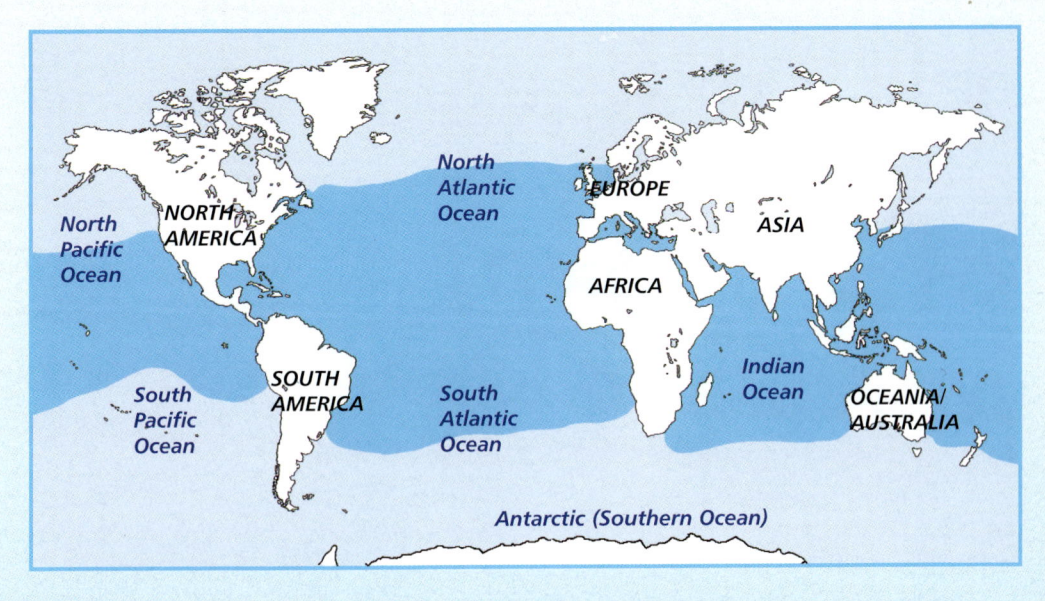

Dolphins can be found in most of the world's oceans. The darker blue band on the map shows where dolphin populations are most dense.

How did the dolphin become a perfect water mammal?
- The dolphin needed to swim, so, over **generations**, its body changed. Dolphins that could swim best survived longer and had more offspring. As a result, over centuries, dolphins' front limbs gradually became flippers and their hind legs disappeared.
- The dolphin still needed to breathe air, just as all mammals, including people, do. Over generations, the dolphin's nostrils moved to the top of its head to form a blowhole that allows it to take in air at the water's surface.
- Like all mammals, the dolphin is warm-blooded. To keep warm in the ocean, the dolphin developed blubber, a layer of fat, to cover its body and serve as **insulation**.

WHERE DO DOLPHINS LIVE?
The dolphin has proved so successful at life that it can be found worldwide in ocean waters that range from warm to freezing cold. Dolphins also live in the rivers of Asia and South America.

There are about forty different **species** of dolphins, which vary in size, shape, and color, depending on where they live.

The Ways of Dolphins

As with all animals, dolphins have a few basic things that they need in order to survive.

GROUP LIVING

An animal that lives in a group is much safer than an animal that lives on its own. The dolphin does not have many enemies in the wild, but it is hunted by sharks and sometimes by killer whales, which are actually a very large kind of dolphin. For safety, dolphins live in groups known as a pods. A shark may try to attack a dolphin, but it rarely succeeds when the dolphin is surrounded by members of its pod.

Often, just fifteen to twenty dolphins live in a pod, but sometimes more than one thousand dolphins live together in one pod! Large pods usually form

Far out to sea, where food is often plentiful, dolphins swim and feed in great numbers.

Dolphins are constantly on the move as they travel to find fresh food supplies.

far out to sea when there is a rich supply of food.

A pod will stay within a **home range**, but pod members do not try to defend their range from other pods. Members of pods come and go as they like, and dolphins may leave one pod to join another.

FINDING FOOD
Dolphins feed on all kinds of fish, squid, octopus, and prawns. A fast-swimming dolphin catches this type of food easily, but a large pod needs plenty of food to eat. A dolphin eats about 14 pounds (6 kilograms) of food a day, so a pod must keep on the move, constantly looking for food supplies. A dolphin can swim as fast as 25 miles (40 kilometers) per hour, but its traveling speed is generally about 5 miles (8 km) per hour. Dolphin pods travel long distances every day, often circling their range, but we do not know the exact distance they cover.

A BREEDING PARTNER
Dolphins need to breed and produce offspring so that there will be future generations. A pod usually includes a number of adult males, known as bulls; adult females, known as cows; and young dolphins, which are called calves. A dolphin may breed with a pod member, but neighboring pods often meet up. These pod meetings provide new opportunities for finding breeding partners. Because dolphin pods do not fight with one another, dolphins have many chances to find new mates.

The Dolphin's Perfect Body

The dolphin spends its entire life in the water, and it is one of the finest swimmers of all the ocean dwellers. Dolphins come in different shapes and sizes, but they are all perfectly **streamlined** to help them swim at fast speeds through the water.

SIZE AND SHAPE
Most species of dolphin measure about 8 to 9 feet (2.45 to 2.75 meters) in length. Hector's dolphin from the coast of New Zealand is the smallest species, measuring just 4.75 feet (1.45 m). Risso's dolphin, a species that is found worldwide, measures about 12 feet (3.65 m) in length.

At the front of its body, a dolphin has flippers, which are used for steering. The power comes from the dolphin's tail, which moves up and down, propelling the dolphin through the water. The tail is divided into two parts, known as flukes. Most dolphins have a **dorsal fin** on the tops of their bodies, which helps them cut through the waves and

The dolphin can swim quickly, and it also has the power to leap out of the water.

8

may also help with balance. Some species, such as the northern right whale dolphin in the northern Pacific, have no dorsal fin.

BLOWHOLE
The dolphin has a small opening on top of its head, known as a blowhole. The dolphin shuts its blowhole when it is underwater and opens the blowhole when it comes to the surface of the water to breathe.

A dolphin surfaces every fifteen to twenty seconds and will clear its blowhole by releasing a spray of water. A dolphin can also dive to depths of 985 feet (300 m) and can stay underwater for up to twenty minutes.

The blowhole can be seen as a tiny opening on the top of the head.

TEETH
A dolphin's teeth are peg-shaped. They are small and sharp, and they are specially designed for catching slippery fish. The number of teeth a dolphin has varies from species to species. Most dolphins have between 100 and 200 teeth, which last throughout their lives.

SKIN
All mammals have hair. A dolphin looks hairless, but dolphins are actually born with tiny mustache hairs that they lose in a few days.

Dolphin bodies are covered with skin that is rubbery to the touch. A layer of blubber under their skin helps keep dolphins warm.

Dolphins come in a variety of colors and markings, which range from solid colors to striped and spotted patterns. A dolphin's body color can work as **camouflage**, which often helps it escape from **predators**. Its camouflaging skin also helps it surprise fish when it is hunting them for food.

How a Dolphin Sees the World

Imagine yourself inside the body of a dolphin and find out how the world would appear if you spent most of your life underwater.

EYESIGHT
Most species of dolphin have good eyesight, both under and above the surface of the water. The dolphin is particularly good at seeing fast-moving objects, which is important when dolphins chase and then catch fish. Most dolphins can see forward, backward, and to the side. Dolphins cannot see upward, which is why they are often seen chasing fish bellyside up.

HEARING
The dolphin's ears are tiny slits that are found just behind the eyes. The dolphin has a very acute sense of hearing and can distinguish high-frequency sounds that we cannot hear. The dolphin takes in sound through its ear slits. Sound also travels from its lower jaw to its inner ear. The sound is then carried to the brain so the dolphin can figure out what the sound means.

The dolphin has good eyesight. It can see underwater and when it comes to the surface.

SMELL

The dolphin has a very poor sense of smell and does not use smell to find food or as a way of communicating with other dolphins.

Many species of dolphin, such as the bottlenose dolphin, have long noses, which are known as beaks. The beak, however, is not used for smelling or breathing. As we have seen, the nostrils are on the top of the head in the form of a blowhole. The beak increases streamlining, and some dolphins use their beaks to search for food on the ocean or river bed.

Dolphins form close friendships, and they will play together and touch each other to show affection.

TASTE

Dolphins can tell the difference between sweet, sour, bitter, and salty flavors. Dolphins use their sense of taste to sample chemicals left in the water by other dolphins. This helps a dolphin to find other dolphins and to discover if a female is ready for breeding. Dolphins also use the ability to "taste" chemical traces to find food. A large **shoal** of fish can leave chemical traces that stay in the water for several hours.

TOUCH

Dolphins are very sensitive to touch. We know that dolphins can sense the water's movements over their bodies, and this sense of touch may be used as a way of finding their way through the ocean's currents. They can sense changes in water pressure, and this information may help them know how deep they are in the ocean. Touch is also used between dolphins as a sign of affection.

Discovering Special skills

The dolphin has a very big brain in relation to its size and it is rated as one of the most intelligent of all animals. Tests have been carried out in zoos and marine parks that show dolphins are quick learners. They use their memories and water skills to perform a wide variety of tricks. How do dolphins use their intelligence in the wild?

WORKING TOGETHER
Dolphins live in family groups, and the pod members help and support each other. Their teamwork is most clearly seen when dolphins are feeding. A group of dolphins work together when they are hunting fish. They use different methods, depending on where they are fishing.

Dolphins work in teams when they are fishing, which makes them far more successful than if they just fished by themselves.

- In open waters, dolphins herd large shoals of fish, circling them and then feasting on them from all sides.
- In shallow waters, dolphins drive fish toward the shore where they have a better chance of catching them than they do in deep water.
- Dolphins also use their bodies to form a wall. When fish are herded toward the dolphin-made barrier, the fish are forced to stop swimming and are easy to catch.
- Dolphins have also learned to swim alongside fishing boats, so they can feed on fish that are thrown overboard by fishermen. The bigger, stronger members of a pod always get the best places to feed.

A dolphin uses a special system called echolocation to steer clear of obstacles, including other dolphins.

SOUND EFFECTS

When a dolphin is swimming deep in the dark ocean or finding its way in muddy river waters, it is often impossible for it to see clearly. A dolphin must swim through plants, steer around rocks, hunt for fish, and avoid other dolphins that are swimming close by.

The dolphin has developed a special system that gives it a picture — in sound — of its water world.

The dolphin makes a series of high-frequency clicks that are too high in pitch for us to hear. Each click hits part of an object in the water, such as a rock or a fish, and bounces back to the dolphin in the form of an echo. This special sound system, which is known as echolocation, can tell a dolphin the shape, size, distance, traveling speed, and location of the object that it is passing.

What Does a Dolphin Do All Day?

Dolphins that live far out in the ocean are very hard to study, but scientists are now developing new techniques, such as fitting satellite transmitters on dolphins, so they can keep track of the dolphins' movements.

ON THE MOVE

Dolphins are very active. They spend about sixteen hours a day on the move, traveling to find food. In the morning, a pod of dolphins usually leaves the shallow offshore waters and heads for deeper water, where the pod is more likely to find shoals of fish.

A small family pod of fifteen to twenty dolphins are not very successful at herding fish, so, as the day passes, neighboring pods meet and work together. A herd of feeding dolphins may include many hundreds of dolphins. Feeding sessions usually last for two to three hours.

If danger threatens, often in the form of a shark or a killer whale, dolphins head for the shoreline, where they can hide in the surf.

PLAYTIME

Dolphins are the most playful of all animals that live in the ocean.

In the morning, a small family pod will move off to deeper water in search of other pods of dolphins with which they can fish.

When a bottlenose dolphin breaches, it can leap 16.5 feet (5 m) from the surface of the water.

Dolphins of all ages enjoy leaping high into the air, launching their whole bodies out of the water, and then landing with mighty splashes. This move is known as **breaching**. The spinner dolphin is famous for the fabulous spins and somersaults it performs in the air.

Dolphins are very curious animals and investigate anything that is new. Dolphins have been seen playing with seaweed, pebbles, and even fish. A dolphin can balance an object on its flippers and then toss it into the air to catch it. Dolphins have also perfected the art of **bow riding**, which is riding the waves at the front, or bow, of a boat or a ship.

SLEEPING

Dolphins need to rest, but they cannot go into a deep sleep because they have to come up to the surface of the water to breathe. Instead, a dolphin will rest for a few minutes at a time on the surface with its blowhole open. At night, the rest periods may extend to seven or eight minutes. Dolphins have the remarkable ability to rest one half of their brains while the other half remains alert in case of danger.

How Do Dolphins Communicate?

Dolphins are very sociable animals. They enjoy being in the company of other dolphins. Dolphins "talk" to each other using a mixed system of sounds and body language. Their ability to communicate with one another helps them cooperate in groups.

DOLPHIN SOUNDS

We have already discovered that dolphins make a series of clicks when they are finding their way about and hunting for fish. A dolphin can make other sounds at the same time, which it uses when it is "talking" to other dolphins.

In a large group, dolphins keep in touch with each other using different types of sound.

If a good supply of fish is found, a dolphin will alert other dolphins in the area by whistling.

Dolphins make a variety of sounds, such as moans, whistles, trills, squeaks, and growls. We are only just beginning to learn the meaning of some of these sounds.

KEEPING IN TOUCH
Whistling is the most important sound that dolphins make when they are communicating with each other. Dolphins whistle tunes that form a complete language only dolphins understand. Whistle sounds carry over long distances, which helps dolphins survive by keeping them together in pods.

Every dolphin has its own individual whistle, which is known as a **signature tune**. Dolphins recognize each other by their signature tunes, and this helps keep a pod together. Dolphins also have long-term friendships with dolphins from neighboring pods. Signatures tunes are used to help recognize individuals and cement friendships with neighbors.

Dolphins not only have their own signature tunes, they also have a special series of whistles they use when talking to members of their own pod. This whistling is like people who live in one area speaking with different accents than people in another area.

Dolphins use whistles in a number of situations:
- When dolphins are traveling together, they keep in touch with whistles.
- When they are hunting for food, dolphins may spread out over a large area. A dolphin whistles to keep in touch with pod members and to signal other dolphins if it comes across a shoal of fish.

- If a shoal of fish is spotted, the dolphins must cooperate with each other as they herd the fish to catch them. Dolphins whistle to one another so they can group themselves in the right positions.
- If danger is spotted, a dolphin whistles to alert all other dolphins in the area.
- A male dolphin attracts the attention of a female with a series of whistles.
- When dolphins meet up at a favorite feeding place, they celebrate with a chorus of whistles.
- When a dolphin is bow riding, pushed along by the power of a boat or a ship, it starts to whistle as a sign of high spirits.

GROUP BUDDIES

Dolphins within a family pod form strong links, joining forces to help and protect each other. Dolphins are affectionate with one another, and pod members sometimes greet each other by rubbing their bodies together. Play also forms a vital part in boosting a kind of team spirit and strengthening ties within a group. Dolphins breach together, leaping out of the water and performing spectacular acrobatics.

If a ship is sighted, a dolphin whistles to alert other dolphins. The dolphins then race to get the best position to ride the waves in front of the ship or play in the frothy surf at the back of the ship. Sailors have enjoyed the company

A dolphin will show off its jumping skills to other dolphins to prove its strength and power.

of playful, cheerful dolphins since people began taking boats into the seas and oceans.

AVOIDING TROUBLE
When dolphins are living together, conflicts can arise if all the pod members are trying to get at the same food supply. Conflict is even more likely to happen when neighboring pods meet up and hundreds of dolphins may gather in a small area.

Dolphins are usually peace-loving animals that do not want to get into fights. For this reason, every dolphin has its own position within a pod and will give way to bigger or more dominant dolphins. When large groups of dolphins meet up, they will use body language to signal to each other, so that low-ranking dolphins can steer clear of any trouble.

Dolphin body language includes:

- Breaching — a dolphin displays its acrobatic skills as a show of strength.
- Lob tailing — a dolphin slaps its tail fluke against the water several times in a row.
- Flipper slapping — a dolphin rolls over at the surface and slaps its flippers in the water.

Dolphins may have other reasons for these body movements. An active, energetic dolphin appears to perform a whole range of movements just for the fun of splashing around in the water!

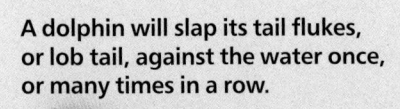

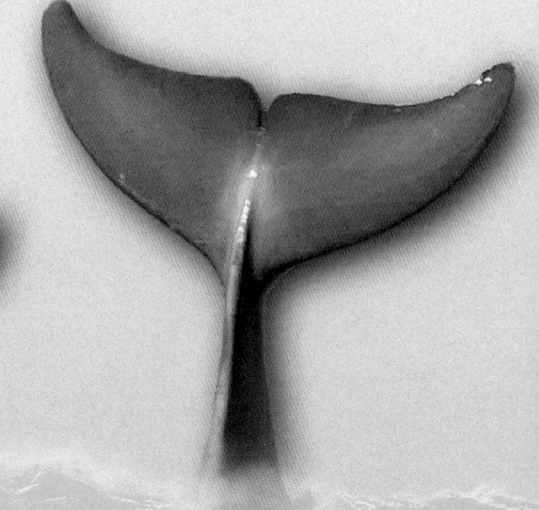

A dolphin will slap its tail flukes, or lob tail, against the water once, or many times in a row.

Times of Trouble

People used to think that dolphins were the greatest peace-keepers of the animal kingdom and that they never got into trouble by fighting each other. By studying dolphins in the wild, however, scientists have discovered that this is not the whole story.

ANGRY DOLPHINS

A low-ranking dolphin usually backs off if it is competing for food with a bigger, stronger dolphin. If two dolphins are evenly matched, however, trouble can break out.

Spinner and bottlenose dolphins have been seen facing up to each other with their mouths wide open. Sometimes, a dolphin makes a growling sound and snaps its jaws open and shut to show how fierce it is. Fights have been seen in the wild, where a dolphin has run its teeth over the back of another dolphin, resulting in a nasty wound. Risso's dolphin is well known for its battered appearance. Its skin is covered in scars, which are caused by the teeth of other Risso's dolphins, and also by bites

Risso's dolphin often has many battle scars covering its body.

The killer whale, or orca, is the greatest enemy of many dolphins. Its huge dorsal fin towers between four and six feet above its back.

from squid, which form an important part of their diet.

Bottlenose dolphins have been spotted attacking smaller species, such as spinner and spotted dolphins. There have also been reports of violent interactions between bottlenose dolphins and harbor porpoises, which are a much smaller type of cetacean. At least one death of a Harbor porpoise that was killed by a bottlenose dolphin has been reported.

DOLPHIN ENEMIES
Dolphins have two enemies to fear in the wild — the shark and the killer whale. The worst shark attacks occur around the coasts of Australia and South Africa. The shark is not always successful. Many dolphins have large scars from shark bites, showing they have survived an attack and have escaped to safety.

Killer whales are another big threat. A killer whale feeds on fish, but it also attacks seals and the smaller species of dolphin.

ILLNESS AND OLD AGE
In the wild, a dolphin lives for twenty-five to thirty years. Very few dolphins survive until they are forty years old. Because dolphins live in pods, they benefit from the support of other members and can rely on the pod to help them find food. Pod members have even been seen trying to help a sick dolphin by swimming alongside it, keeping it close to the surface so it can breathe and try to recover.

When Dolphins Are Ready to Breed

Dolphins live their lives surrounded by other dolphins, so finding a breeding partner is not very difficult.

READY TO BREED

A female (cow) dolphin is ready to breed when she is about eight years old. Males (bulls) are usually a little older before they are ready to compete for cows. Adult bulls and cows look identical. The only way to tell them apart is to look at their undersides. A cow has two small slits on either side, which are the openings for **mammary glands**. These produce milk when a cow is nursing a baby dolphin, or calf.

CHANGING PARTNERS

Most species of dolphin breed at all times of the year. A bull dolphin can taste chemicals left in the water by a cow that is ready to breed, and he will follow her trail. Dolphins do not breed only with members of their own pod, because the pod usually does not have

Bulls may compete with each other by leaping and showing off to win a breeding partner.

22

The pair will spend a brief time together and then the bull will swim away, leaving the cow to be a single mom.

enough unrelated partners to choose from. When large groups of dolphins gather to feed, they use the opportunity to find breeding partners.

Sometimes, bulls compete for the same cow. The bulls usually try to win the cow's affection by showing off their strength, leaping high into the air. The bull then moves close to the cow, and the pair will have a brief **courtship**, swimming together and stroking each other with their flippers.

Once dolphins have **mated**, the bull swims away and will take no part in raising the calf. A cow has many different breeding partners throughout her life, and there is no lasting bond between bulls and cows that have produced offspring.

WAITING GAME
After mating, a cow is pregnant for twelve months before she gives birth. In the animal kingdom, twelve months is a very long pregnancy. It is three months longer than for a human baby. The reason for the long pregnancy is that calves born in the deep ocean cannot be helpless. A calf must be able to swim from the moment it is born.

The Family Life of Dolphins

Dolphin calves are born in the greatest secrecy. Very few births have been seen in the wild. Most of our information comes from watching the birth of dolphin calves in zoos.

GIVING BIRTH

Like all mammals, dolphins give birth to live young. A single calf will be born. It is very rare for a dolphin to give birth to twins. If this happens, one of the calves will die, as the mother dolphin is not able to raise two calves at once.

When a cow is ready to give birth, she heads for the shallow coastal waters. One or more female "helpers" usually goes with her. The helpers protect the pregnant cow from predators while she is giving birth. They also help the baby after it is born and learning to swim.

The calf is born tail first. Within seconds after it is born, the mother

The calf keeps close to its mother as it swims through the ocean waters.

For the first six months, a calf will feed entirely on milk from its mother.

and her helpers guide the calf to the surface of the water so it can take its first breath of air.

A newborn calf measures about 39 to 53 inches (100 to 135 centimeters) in length, and weighs 22 to 44 pounds (10 to 20 kg), which is about ten percent of its mother's weight. To begin with, the calf is unsteady in the water, but, within thirty minutes, it will be swimming very well.

The calf will then drink milk from its mother. A dolphin's milk is very rich in fat, which helps the calf grow quickly. The calf needs to be fed every thirty minutes.

To nurse, the calf slips its tongue inside its mother's mammary slit and wraps it around the mother's nipple. The calf nurses underwater. This means that both the calf and mother must hold their breath while nursing. To help her calf nurse quickly, the cow can squirt milk from her mammary glands.

LIFE IN THE POD
The calf stays close to its mother for safety. The calf has another reason to stay by its mother's side. The calf is pulled along in the water by the power of its mother's swimming movements, which create a strong current. This current saves the calf from using up most of its energy while swimming.

The pod members take a great interest in new calves, and a couple of females will help raise the calf.

The Calves Grow Up

Dolphin calves make easy meals for sharks and killer whales. Calves do not swim as fast as adult dolphins, and they do not try to defend themselves. For these reasons, adult dolphins keep a close watch on calves as they are growing up. Even so, many calves die before becoming adults. In some species, 50 percent of the calves do not make it to adulthood. The calves of older, more experienced cows have the best chance of surviving.

PLAYING AND LEARNING

A dolphin calf starts to eat fish from about three to six months of age, but milk remains an important part of its diet for some time. Most dolphin calves continue nursing from their mothers until they are eighteen months old.

During this time, a mother dolphin gives most of her attention to her calf. She stays close to the calf at all times, teaching it everything she knows. A dolphin calf learns by copying its mother.

Dolphins are devoted mothers, and for two years, they will protect their calves from danger and teach them how to survive.

When a dolphin is fully grown, it is time to leave the family pod.

It also learns by copying other dolphins in the pod.

Dolphin calves play with adults as well as with other calves. Play gives a calf the chance to improve its swimming and hunting skills as it chases other dolphins and leaps out of the water. Dolphin calves are very curious. They investigate anything new. They play with pebbles and shells and are good at problem solving.

GOING SOLO

A young dolphin is able to look after itself by the age of two years. By this time, its mother will be ready to start breeding again. One of the most important signs that a dolphin is becoming fully independent is when it develops its own signature tune. Most dolphins do this by the time they are two years old. At this point, other dolphins learn to recognize the youngster as an individual in its own right. Males may copy the signature of their mother. Sharing the same signature tune helps them instantly recognize each other in years to come. This shared tune will keep them from breeding with each other.

When a dolphin is two to three years of age, it will usually leave its pod and find other dolphins its own age. These dolphin groups are known as juvenile pods. In most cases, the young dolphins will stay together until they are old enough to start breeding. Then, the females will rejoin their mothers' pods. The males will usually stay with the males of the juvenile pod.

Dolphins and People

The dolphin is a highly successful animal. It has different species spread all over the world. Because it is protected by living in a group and having few natural enemies, the dolphin faces few dangers except those introduced by people.

THE HUNTED

For centuries, people have hunted dolphins for their meat. Many countries now have laws that protect dolphins, but in Japan and South America, dolphins are still hunted with nets, rifles, and hand-held **harpoons**. Hundreds of dolphins are killed every year when they become tangled in fishing nets.

One of the greatest threats to dolphins is a fishing method known as **purse seining.** When this method is used to catch tuna, many dolphins can be accidently caught and killed in the process. In the most modern version of purse seining, a helicopter circles the ocean in areas that are rich in tuna. When dolphins are spotted, the helicopter follows them. As

Swimming with dolphins is now a great tourist attraction. This activity shows how well people and dolphins can live together.

The world's oceans must be kept clean so that dolphins always have a place to live and breed.

soon as the dolphins find tuna, the fishermen cast a huge net around the dolphins and the fish. The net can be up to one mile (1.6 km) long. The sides of the net are pulled like the sides of a drawstring purse, and the catch is lifted clear of the water. Unfortunately, many dolphins become tangled in the net and drown. Calves may become separated from their mothers and will often die. This fishing method kills about 20,000 dolphins a year.

DIRTY WATERS
For dolphins to be healthy and find enough food to eat, the water they live in must be clean. Today, much seawater, particularly near coasts, is becoming increasingly **polluted** in some parts of the world. Raw, untreated **sewage** is pumped into sea and ocean waters every day. Industrial waste, which may contain poisonous chemicals, is also dumped in the seas and oceans. The worst disaster is when an oil tanker spills its load and vast areas of the sea are transformed into a sticky, poisonous oil slick.

Many groups and governments are working to solve the problems of water pollution. If plants and small fish fail to survive in the ocean, there will be no food for dolphins and the other ocean predators. Dolphins also die from swallowing human garbage that has drifted out to sea, such as rubber tires, plastic bags, and plastic bottles.

A BRIGHTER FUTURE
At the present time, river dolphins are the only species that are threatened with **extinction**. Many people believe we must act now to protect the dolphin so that future generations can enjoy this amazing animal living in the wild.

Glossary

bow riding gliding along in the waves at the bow (front) of a boat or ship

breaching leaping up so that most of the body is out of the water

camouflage body colors and marks that blend in with the surroundings

courtship a time of getting to know each other before a male and female get ready to mate

dorsal fin the fin on the back of a dolphin's body

extinction the complete disappearance of a living organism

generations different age groups within a population of related animals, such as grandparents, parents, and chidren

harpoons barbed spears used to hunt whales, dolphins, and fish

home range an area where a pod of dolphins or other animals live

insulation a covering to prevent the loss of heat

mammals warm-blooded animals that have hair and give birth to live young that are nursed with milk produced by their mothers

mammary glands the glands on a female mammal that produce milk

mated the act of two animals that joined together to breed

polluted dirty and unhealthy

porpoises the smallest members of the cetacean family. They look much like dolphins, but they have sharper, chisel-shaped teeth.

predators meat-eating hunters

purse seining a fishing method that uses an open-bottomed net that can be pulled closed after fish have entered. It is lifted out of the water like a purse.

sewage human waste that is carried away in a system of pipes called sewers

shoal a large group of fish

signature tune a dolphin's personal identity whistle

species animals with similar characteristics that can only breed with each other

streamlined having bodies shaped to travel with the least resistance to air, wind, or water

whales the largest cetaceans

More Books to Read

Dolphins. Creatures of the Sea (series). Kris Hirschmann (Kid Haven Press)

Dolphins. Our Wild World (series). Julia Vogel (Northwood Press)

Everything Dolphin: What Kids Really Want to Know about Dolphins. Kids Faqs (series). Marty Crisp (Northwood Press)

Little Dolphins. Born to be Wild (series). Valerie Guidoux (Gareth Stevens Publishing)

Wild About Dolphins. Nicola Davies (Candlewick Press)

Web Sites

All About Dolphins
teacher.scholastic.com/dolphin/about.htm

Dolphins: Close Encounters
www.pbs.org/wnet/nature/dolphins/

National Geographic Creature Feature Bottlenose Dolphins
www.nationalgeographic.com/kids/creature_feature/0108/dolphins.html

World Almanac Dolphins
www.worldalmanacforkids.com/explore/animals/dolphin.html

Publisher's note to educators and parents: Our editors have carefully reviewed these Web sites to ensure that they are suitable for children. Many Web sites change frequently, however, and we cannot guarantee that a site's future contents will continue to meet our high standards of quality and educational value. Be advised that children should be closely supervised whenever they access the Internet.

Index

birthing 23–24
blowhole 5, 9, 11, 15
blubber 5, 9
bottlenose dolphins 11, 15, 20, 21
bow riding 15, 18
breaching 15, 18, 19
breeding 7, 11, 22–23, 27, 29
bulls 7, 22, 23

calves 7, 23, 24–27, 29
cetaceans 4, 21
conflicts 19, 20–21
cows 7, 22, 23, 24, 25, 26

diving 9
dolphin colors 5, 9
dorsal fin 8, 9, 21

echolocation 13
enemies 6, 21, 26, 28
extinction 29
eyesight 10

fighting 7, 19–21
flippers 8
flukes 8, 19
food 6, 7, 9, 11, 14, 17, 19, 20, 21, 29

hearing 10
home range 7
hunting 12–14

juvenile pods 27

killer whales 6, 14, 21, 26
lob tailing 19
old age 21
play 4, 11, 14–15, 18, 26, 27
pods 6–7, 12, 13, 14. 17, 18, 19, 21, 22, 25, 27
pollution 29
porpoises 4, 21

Risso's dolphins 8, 20
river dolphins 5, 29

sharks 6, 14, 21, 26
signature tunes 17, 27
size 5, 8, 25
sleep 15
smell, sense of 11
sounds 10, 13, 16–18, 27
spinner dolphins 15, 20, 21
spotted dolphins 21

taste, sense of 11
teeth 9, 20
touch, sense of 11

whales 4
whistles 17–18, 27

HPARX + 599 .53 B

Friends of the
Houston Public Library

**BARNES, JULIA,
THE SECRET LIVES OF
DOLPHINS
PARK PLACE
11/07**